Dangerous Creatures

of the
Forests and Woodlands

Helen Bateman and Jayne Denshire

Smart Apple Media

Smart Apple Media
1980 Lookout Drive
North Mankato
Minnesota 56003

First published in 2005 by
MACMILLAN EDUCATION AUSTRALIA PTY LTD
627 Chapel Street, South Yarra 3141

Visit our website at www.macmillan.com.au

Associated companies and representatives throughout the world.

Library of Congress Cataloging-in-Publication Data

Bateman, Helen.
  Of the forests and woodlands / by Helen Bateman and Jayne Denshire.
  p. cm. – (Dangerous creatures)
  Includes index.

  ISBN 1-58340-766-9

  1. Forest animals—Juvenile literature. 2. Dangerous animals—Juvenile literature.
  I. Denshire, Jayne. II. Title.
  QL112.B36 2005
  691.73—dc22

                                                    2005042867

Project management by Limelight Press Pty Ltd
Design by Stan Lamond, Lamond Art & Design
Illustrations by Edwina Riddell
Maps by Laurie Whiddon, Map Illustrations. Adapted by Lamond Art & Design
Research by Kate McAllan

Consultant: George McKay PhD, Conservation Biologist

Printed in China

Acknowledgments
The authors and the publisher are grateful to the following for permission to reproduce copyright material:

Cover photograph: funnel-web spider, courtesy of Peter Marsack/Lochman Transparencies

Fredy Mercay ANTPhoto.com p. 19; N.H.P.A./ANTPhoto.com p. 17; Otto Roge/ANTPhoto. com p. 28; Ferrero-Labat/AUSCAPE p. 26; APL/Corbis/Oriol Almany p. 20; APL/Corbis/Niall Benvie p. 24; APL/Corbis/B. Borrell Casals p. 9; Australian Picture Library/Corbis p. 16; APL/Corbis/David Hosking pp. 11, 18; APL/Corbis/George McCarthy p. 21; APL/Premium Animals & Nature 2 p. 13; APL/Rob Watkins p. 15; APL/Corbis/Staffan Widstrand p. 27; Corbis p. 7 (top left); Getty Images/Art Wolfe p. 12; Jiri Lochman/Lochman Transparencies pp. 13 (top), 14; Peter Marsack/Lochman Transparencies pp. 22, 23; Dave Watts/Lochman Transparencies p. 5; Nature Scenes PhotoDisc p. 5; Paolo De Oliveira/Photolibrary.com p. 29; Robin Redfern/Photolibrary.com p. 25; George Reszeter/Photolibrary.com p. 10; Tom Soucek/Photolibrary.com p. 7 (top right).

Please note
At the time of printing, the Internet addresses appearing in this book were correct. Owing to the dynamic nature of the Internet, however, we cannot guarantee that all these addresses will remain correct.

Contents

When a word is printed in **bold**, you can look up its meaning in the Glossary on page 31.

Life in the forests and woodlands

There are forests and woodlands in many countries around the world. Some of these are **evergreen,** and grow mostly where the summers are hot and the winters are not too cold. Other forests are **deciduous,** which means that most of the trees lose their leaves in winter. They are found mostly in Europe, North America, and Asia where the winters are cold and the summers are warm. However, forests of conifers, which have extra tough leaves, also grow where the winters are very cold.

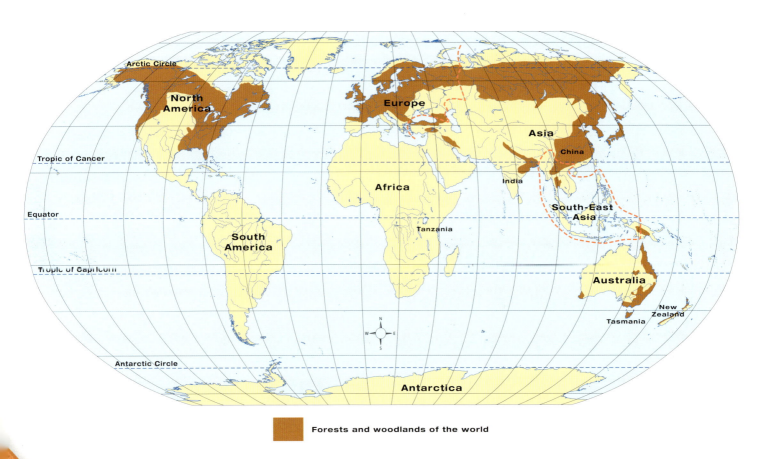

Forests and woodlands of the world

▲ **Forests and woodlands grow in a wide range of climates where there is plenty of rain. Many of the evergreen forests are found in areas where the winters are warmer. Many of the deciduous forests are found in areas where the winters are colder.**

4

▶ There is plenty of plant food in forests and woodlands, but growth usually slows down in winter. This is when survival becomes even more dangerous.

lynx

Level 4

bear

owl

Level 3

fox

spider

Level 2

squirrel

bird

Level 1

forest plants and shrubs

▲ The forests and woodlands food chain has four links. The animals from each level survive by eating the animals from the level below.

Danger and survival

Animals living in forests and woodlands behave dangerously because they need to survive in their **habitat**. All creatures have to find food and shelter and often need to defend themselves against other animals at the same time. For many creatures, it is a case of kill or be killed.

In forests and woodlands, some creatures live on plants, but most have to hunt and eat other animals to survive. Some creatures are dangerous to humans, but usually only if they feel threatened by them.

The natural **food chain** of the forests and woodlands begins with plants and shrubs. These are eaten by animals such as spiders, birds, and squirrels, which all belong to the second level of the chain. The next level is those animals, such as foxes and owls, that eat the plant-eaters. On the highest level of the food chain are the top **predators** of the forests and woodlands, such as grizzly bears and lynxes.

Grizzly bears

VITAL STATISTICS

LENGTH
up to 11 feet (3.2 m)

WEIGHT
up to one ton (1 t)

WHERE FOUND
North America

The grizzly bears of North America are one of the world's most dangerous creatures. They are heavy, powerful animals with huge, curved claws, and sharp teeth. The brown fur on their back and shoulders often has white, silvery tips. This gives them a grizzled, or gray-haired, appearance and has led to their name.

Grizzly bears usually run away from people, but not always. They are unpredictable, and will attack humans, especially if they feel their cubs are threatened. Hikers are often told to make a lot of noise to scare grizzlies off, but this does not always work. Sometimes the noise can actually attract them.

A mixed diet

Grizzlies eat both plants and meat. Most of the meat they eat comes from dead animals they find, but they are hunters as well as **scavengers**. Grizzly bears are at their most dangerous when they have their young with them, or when they are eating their food. Because of their size, grizzlies have few predators, but they turn on each other, especially to fight for food.

◀ A grizzly bear stands up on its hind legs, not to attack, but to get a better view.

◄ Grizzly bears have short, small teeth at the front of their mouth for eating berries and plants, and large, sharp teeth at the side and back for eating meat.

Large and lethal

Grizzly bears hunt moose, elk, mountain sheep, and goats. They have sharp hearing and a good sense of smell. Grizzly bears often wait in hiding for their **prey**. They are fast runners, using their speed to chase their victim and then their strength to knock it down when they catch up. One blow from a grizzly's paw can break an animal's skull, and a grizzly's jaws are powerful enough to bite through an animal's leg.

▲ Grizzly bears fight over favorite hunting spots.

DANGER REPORT

In September, 2004, a 67-year-old man was hunting with friends in Colorado when he came across a female grizzly bear and her two cubs. The man fired a shot to alert his friends and get their help. The man tried to fight the bear off, but she bit first his head and then his hand as he tried to protect himself. The bear pushed him over, but lost interest in him when the man pretended to be dead. The man, who was rescued, said he did not blame the bear because she was only protecting her cubs.

fact flash

Grizzly bears are experts at catching salmon.

Stone centipedes

VITAL STATISTICS

LENGTH
up to one inch (3 cm)

WHERE FOUND
worldwide

Stone centipedes, which are also called common centipedes or brown centipedes, are found in forests and woodlands all around the world. They live under leaf litter, bark, rotting wood, and rocks. In summer, stone centipedes burrow into the soil to stay moist. They can live up to three years.

Stone centipedes are fierce, **carnivorous** predators, but they are not aggressive to humans. They usually try to escape rather than fight, but they will give humans a painful bite if they are disturbed and accidentally handled.

Legs to spare

Stone centipedes have 14 pairs of legs when they first hatch, but they grow another pair as they become adults. Their long **antennae** are harmless. They have a flattish body, a small mouth, strong jaws, and large claws, or **fangs**, which they use to inject **venom** into their victim.

fact flash

If a centipede loses a leg it can grow another one to replace it.

fact flash

When centipedes walk, they have only one leg in eight on the ground at any one time.

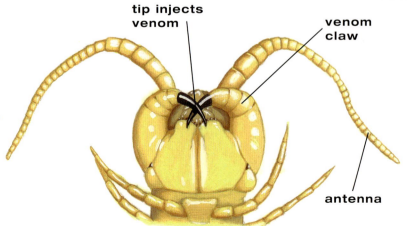

▶ Stone centipedes produce venom in special glands in their head. They inject it into their prey through their claws.

tip injects venom

venom claw

antenna

▼ Stone centipedes hold their victim still with their strong claws and chew it into small pieces.

On the prowl

Stone centipedes prowl around at night, hunting insects, spiders, worms, and even other centipedes. They are very fast crawlers. Stone centipedes have poor eyesight, so they use their sensitive antennae to help them to find their prey. When they find their victim, they grab it with their claws and paralyze it with venom. When their prey becomes paralyzed, they use their jaws to slice it into pieces small enough to swallow.

fact flash

Stone centipedes can crawl backward almost as easily as forward.

Eurasian cuckoos

VITAL STATISTICS

LENGTH
up to 13 inches
(33 cm)

WEIGHT
up to three ounces
(90 g)

WHERE FOUND
Europe, Asia, Africa

Eurasian cuckoos are medium-sized birds with black and white feathers, and long, pointed wings. They hunt and eat spiders, beetles, moths, butterflies, and especially hairy caterpillars that other birds avoid. Eurasian cuckoos are also dangerous because they are **parasites**. They use other birds by forcing them to care for them and feed them. To do this successfully, they kill off many of the other birds' chicks.

Sneaky move

Eurasian cuckoos lay their eggs in the nests of other birds, such as reed warblers, and white wagtails. The mother cuckoo chooses a nest, waits until the owners are away, then flies down to lay her own egg. The mother cuckoo often destroys any eggs already in the nest to make sure that her chick will get all the attention and food from its foster parents.

▲ The back of a cuckoo chick is cup-shaped to help it push other eggs out of the nest.

Clever cuckoos

Eurasian cuckoos can even change the look of their eggs so they look similar to those already in the nest. Sometimes the foster parents notice that the egg is not theirs and try to destroy it, but cuckoo eggs are much tougher than other eggs and are difficult to break.

Often the foster parents lay more eggs of their own after the mother cuckoo has laid hers, but these new eggs are still not safe. Eurasian cuckoo eggs develop and hatch much faster than other birds' eggs. When they do hatch, the young cuckoo pushes the other chicks and eggs out of the nest. The foster parents have no choice but to feed the cuckoo chick.

◄ After she has chosen a nest, the mother cuckoo gets rid of any eggs already in there.

Wild boars

VITAL STATISTICS

LENGTH
up to seven feet (2 m) (including tail)

WEIGHT
up to 441 pounds (200 k)

WHERE FOUND
Europe, Asia, and North Africa

There are 16 types of wild boar living worldwide. The wild boars of Europe live in forests eating leaves, grass, and a wide variety of small creatures. Wild boars are not aggressive to humans, but they will attack if they feel threatened, particularly if they are with their young.

Tough teeth

Wild boars are very dangerous because of their **tusks**. These are extra-large teeth that grow out of their mouth and curve over their top lip. The tusks on males can grow to nearly five inches (13 cm).

In the breeding season, males fight for a female. They become very aggressive, bumping and shoving each other, standing up on their hind legs and foaming at the mouth. If this does not scare one of them off, they attack with their tusks, trying to slash open each other's side.

▲ A wild boar's tusks are hollow at the base. They keep growing right through the animal's life.

DANGER REPORT

In March, 2003, six people were injured, two seriously, by a wild boar in a forest region in Shizuoka, Japan. One victim suffered a broken bone caused by the charging pig, and another was bitten in five places on the legs. Witnesses said the wild boar was about five feet (1.5 m) in length and about 287 pounds (130 kg) in weight.

▲ Female wild boars have tusks, but they are much smaller than those of the males.

A nose for the job

Wild boars use their extraordinary sense of smell to hunt lizards, baby birds, insects, worms, frogs, rabbits, mice, and snakes. They also eat dead animals. They do not have good eyesight, but their hearing is excellent.

Wild boars are dangerous to humans, especially if the humans disturb them when they are eating, or if a **sow** thinks her piglets are in danger. They are very fast runners and will attack humans, charging at them and using their tusks to defend their territory.

▲ Wild boar piglets have striped coats that help them hide in the thick grass.

Spotted-tailed quolls

VITAL STATISTICS

LENGTH
up to four feet
(1.3 m) (including tail)

WEIGHT
up to 15 pounds
(7 kg)

WHERE FOUND
Tasmania, and east
coast of mainland
Australia

Spotted-tailed quolls are the second largest of the carnivorous **marsupials** alive today. They look a little like a large cat with a long tail. They are fierce predators of other creatures, and will certainly attack a human if they are cornered. Their sharp teeth and claws can inflict serious wounds that can easily become infected. They are just as fierce when they are defending their territory and will fight animals much larger than themselves.

▲ Spotted-tailed quolls become independent hunters at the early age of four months. They quickly become successful at catching prey without any training from their parents.

14

▲ Spotted-tailed quolls have large canine teeth shaped like daggers that they use to hold their prey.

Rest time

During the day, spotted-tailed quolls rest in hollow logs and rock crevices. They mark off their own patch of territory from other quolls with urine and **dung**. They usually hunt alone at night, tracking their prey by following its scent trails.

Speed and balance

Spotted-tailed quolls hunt possums, wallabies, bandicoots, reptiles, and insects on the forest floor, where they quickly run them down. Spotted-tailed quolls also hunt in trees, where they leap on birds that are resting in their nests at night. They knock the birds to the ground, but they are able to keep a firm hold on the tree themselves because their feet have ridges specially developed for gripping. They are excellent climbers and will often pursue their prey into trees.

Spotted-tailed quolls grab their victims in their front paws. They kill larger animals by a powerful bite to the back of the head and neck with their large **canine teeth**. Then they use their sharp, cutting side teeth to slice into the meat. They kill smaller animals, such as insects, by crushing them.

15

Fire salamanders

VITAL STATISTICS

LENGTH
up to 11 inches
(28 cm)

WHERE FOUND
Northwest Africa,
western Asia, and
Europe

Fire salamanders are **amphibians** that live near streams in damp forests and woodlands. They are slow-moving hunters that usually hide under logs and rocks during the day to keep moist. They defend themselves with a poison that paralyzes their prey and is also dangerous to humans.

Hot and cold

Fire salamanders cannot survive in extremely hot or cold temperatures. In places with very cold winters, they **hibernate** in caves or under the ground, using the same place each year. They usually come out at night to hunt creatures with soft bodies, such as worms, flies, or millipedes. They also eat insect **larvae**.

fact flash

The fire salamander's black and brilliant yellow or orange markings are a warning to predators not to attack.

Using their senses

If there is some light, fire salamanders can use their sight to detect their prey. If there is not much light, they find prey using their sense of smell, but they can only catch it by smell if it stays still. They slowly approach their victim, then quickly grab it at the last moment.

▼ The skin of a fire salamander is shiny, smooth, and rubbery looking.

fact flash

All fire salamanders have a black body with yellow or orange markings, but fire salamanders from different areas have different patterns.

Ready, aim, fire

When they are in danger, fire salamanders squirt their attacker with poison, which they produce in glands behind their eyes and along their body. They can squirt an attacker more than seven feet (2 m) away. The poison is quite powerful, so that even touching the skin of a fire salamander can make animals and humans sick.

▲ **A fire salamander grabs its prey in its teeth, and swallows it whole, without breaking it apart.**

Powerful owls

VITAL STATISTICS

LENGTH
up to 26 inches
(65 cm)

WEIGHT
up to four pounds
(1.7 kg)

WINGSPAN
up to five feet (1.5 m)

WHERE FOUND
southeastern
Australia

Powerful owls are the largest owls in Australia. They are fierce hunters of a wide variety of animals and will attack humans, especially if the humans disturb their nesting area. Powerful owls are usually found in male and female pairs in forest gullies. They do not always roost together, but they are always close enough so that they can hear each other call in times of danger.

Powerful owls have a sharp, hooked beak, strong legs and feet, and sharp, curved **talons**. They have very keen eyesight, and their excellent hearing means they can also hunt in almost complete darkness.

Finding food

Powerful owls begin to hunt at dusk. They hunt from their perches on high branches, swooping down to grab their prey with their talons. Their wings and feathers are softer and looser than other birds, which means they can fly more gently and more silently to surprise their victim.

▲ Powerful owls have large eyes to help them see in low-light conditions.

► Powerful owls often carry part of their prey back to their nest. They drape it over a branch and hold it in a talon all day, then eat it just before they set out again to hunt the next evening.

A large meal

Powerful owls hunt quite large prey, including ring-tailed possums, gliders, flying foxes and young brush-tailed possums, rabbits, rats, and cats. They also hunt large birds, such as magpies, ravens, and kookaburras. The owls often attack these birds when they are quietly resting in their nest at night.

Eating methods

Powerful owls eat their victim starting at the head, and often they swallow it whole. If they do swallow it whole, they **regurgitate** the parts they cannot digest, such as bones, fur, and feathers. Sometimes they tear their prey apart using their long, sharp beak. Often, they eat only part of the victim, leaving the tail and the back legs.

Common adders

VITAL STATISTICS

LENGTH
up to 35 inches
(90 cm)

WHERE FOUND
Europe, central and
eastern Asia

Common adders are the only venomous snakes in northwest Europe. They are often called European adders or common vipers. They have a heavy body and a large head. Common adders are keen hunters, but they prefer to remain hidden unless they are looking for food. They are dangerous to humans usually only if humans disturb them, or try to catch them.

Limited season

Some common adders live in very cold areas, and so are active for only a few months each year when it is warm. They have to eat a lot so that they can build up enough fat to survive on when they hibernate during the winter months. They hunt small **mammals** such as rats and mice, and also hunt lizards, frogs, and birds.

fact flash

Some common adders hibernate for up to eight months a year.

Sit and wait

Common adders usually lie in wait and **ambush** their prey. Their venom is quite strong and will easily kill small animals. With humans, however, although the venom causes them a lot of pain and swelling, common adders do not inject enough of it to cause death.

◄ The zigzag skin pattern of the common adder helps it blend perfectly with its environment.

fact flash

Common adders swallow their prey whole, starting at the head.

Death trap

Common adders first strike with their fangs to inject their venom and then they release the animal. This means that the snake does not waste its energy holding on to its struggling victim. Common adders have an excellent sense of smell, so they simply follow the victim's scent trail until they find the dead or dying animal, and then they start to eat it.

▲ Male common adders fight each other for the right to mate with a female. They twist around each other and wrestle, trying to push each other's head downward.

Funnel-web spiders

VITAL STATISTICS

LENGTH
up to one inch
(3 cm)

WHERE FOUND
eastern Australia

There are 36 species of funnel-web spider in eastern Australia, all of which are fierce hunters. The most dangerous to humans is the Sydney funnel-web. Funnel-web spiders are large, dark-colored spiders with massive fangs up to 0.3 inch (7 mm) long. They make their burrows in damp, sheltered locations, such as under rocks or rotting logs in woodlands and forests.

▲ Funnel-web spiders rear up when they are angry because they can only strike downward with their fangs.

Spinning silk

Funnel-web spiders spin a pocket of white silk with thin threads around, and stretching out from, the entrance of their burrow. These threads vibrate when they are touched by prey, such as a mouse, lizard, frog, or bird. The spider waits just inside the nest for this signal. It then rushes out and pounces on the victim, striking down on it with its fangs. The spider's venom paralyzes the prey and the spider drags it into its burrow to be eaten.

Deadly rage

Funnel-web spiders are not aggressive toward humans unless they are cornered or annoyed. Their venom is extremely toxic to humans and leads quickly to **suffocation** and heart failure unless an **antivenin** is given. The bite is instantly painful and spreads quickly through the body. When a human is bitten, the fangs are often driven so deeply into the skin that the spider has to be torn away.

fact flash

The fangs of funnel-web spiders are large. They are sharp enough to pierce the skulls of small lizards and frogs, and the hard shells of insects.

▶ Unlike other spiders, the venom of male funnel-webs is more dangerous for humans than that of the female.

Pine martens

▼ Pine martens
usually live on
their own, and
will fight each
other over food.

Pine martens are members of the weasel family. They live in dens in thick forests and woodlands where dense tree cover protects them from predators. Each marten marks off its territory with dung, or **scats**, so other martens know they should stay away. Pine martens look a little like a cat. They have long, dark brown fur with a yellowy bib and a bushy tail. They are fierce hunters of many small animals, but they are not dangerous to humans.

fact flash

Pine martens can leap over gaps of up to 12 feet (3.5 m) between trees.

Evening meal

Pine martens hunt mostly at night and their main prey is small **rodents**, rabbits, hares, frogs, and reptiles. They also eat insects, snails, and worms as well as berries and nuts. They have been known to scavenge as well.

Pine martens are very fast and **agile**. They can chase squirrels through the trees and catch them. Sometimes they slip on the soft bark, but if they fall, they usually manage to twist themselves around so that they land safely on all four feet.

side
tooth

canine
tooth

▲ Pine martens
have sharp side teeth and
long canines to help them
hold their prey. Their side
teeth are used to slice meat.

▼ A pine marten's long, bushy tail helps it balance as it leaps from branch to branch.

Lone hunters

Pine martens usually hunt alone during winter as well as summer. They often **stalk** their prey and then make a sudden rush at it, either on the ground, or from a tree by running down tree trunks headfirst. They grab on to their victim with their curved, sharp claws and kill it by biting it, usually around the back of the neck.

fact flash

A female pine marten drives the male away after they mate. She raises the young alone.

Eurasian lynxes

VITAL STATISTICS

LENGTH
up to five feet (1.55 m)

WEIGHT
up to 84 pounds
(38 kg)

WHERE FOUND
northern Europe and
down to eastern Asia

Eurasian lynxes are the largest of the lynx cats. They live in cool forests and thick scrub where they can hide in the undergrowth. In winter, they hide behind rocks. Their thick fur protects them from the cold. During severe storms they shelter in caves. They are skilful, deadly hunters, but they are also shy animals, and they avoid contact with humans if possible.

▲ Eurasian lynxes hunt smaller animals such as hares when larger prey is scarce.

▲ Lynxes have specially shaped long ears that give them an extraordinary sense of hearing.

Lone hunters

Eurasian lynxes hunt alone, usually at dawn and dusk. They hunt several species of small deer, as well as hares, rabbits, squirrels, birds, and mice. They have even been known to attack domestic sheep and goats. They hunt their prey using their keen eyesight and excellent hearing. Then they use their sharp claws, powerful jaws, and long, pointed canine teeth to kill it. Eurasian lynxes often bury any uneaten prey and come back the next day to finish it off.

Sneak attack

Eurasian lynxes sometimes stalk their prey, getting as close as they can before pouncing on it. Other times they hide and wait for the prey to come near them. Their coloring is excellent **camouflage**. They can run very fast, but only for short distances. Eurasian lynxes are amazing jumpers, and can bring down animals that are four times bigger than themselves. First they grab their victim with their front claws. Then they grip the animal's neck in their jaws and kill it with one bite.

European wasps

VITAL STATISTICS

LENGTH
up to 0.6 inch (1.5 cm)

WHERE FOUND
Europe, North Africa, and western Asia. Introduced to Australia and New Zealand

▼ Unlike honeybees that die when they have used their sting, European wasps can use their sting many times.

European wasps are called "social" wasps. This means that they live in a **colony** and work together to raise their young. They have a queen who lays eggs and who is cared for by the worker bees. The workers also clean the eggs and feed the larvae with insects. European wasps make their nest in logs or holes in the ground.

In Europe when winter arrives, the workers die off and the queen goes into hibernation. In Australia, the winters are not cold enough to kill the workers, so the queen keeps on laying eggs. This is why nests in Australia are so large. European wasps are very aggressive and will attack any human who disturbs their nest, sometimes stinging them through their clothing.

A sting in the tail

European wasps use the sting in their tail to inject venom that paralyzes and subdues their prey so that they can carry it back to the nest. They also use it to defend their nest against intruders. Only the female worker wasps can sting. The part of their body that would lay eggs if they were the queen develops into a stinger instead.

fact flash

European wasp nests in Australia can hold as many as 100,000 wasps.

Hunting together

European wasps hunt spiders, caterpillars, and other insects. When they sting, they send off a scent that encourages other European wasps to join them in the attack.

For humans, the sting of a European wasp is much more painful than a bee sting. Some humans are allergic to the venom. They can become very sick or even go into shock and die if they are stung. The attack is more likely to be fatal if the person is stung a number of times.

▲ The worker European wasps carry their paralyzed prey in their legs back to the nest.

DANGER REPORT

In June, 2001, in a bushland town in Victoria, Australia, an eight-year-old girl was attacked by European wasps and bitten 50 times. The girl's clothes and hair were covered in wasps. A neighbor had to hose her down to force the wasps off her, and to stop them from stinging her further. The girl was taken to hospital and treated with antivenin.

Endangered animals
of the
forests and woodlands

More than 5,000 animal species in the world today are endangered. They are in danger from their competitors and predators, and they are in danger from natural disasters, such as droughts, floods, and fires.

But the greatest threat to animals comes from the most dangerous animals of all—humans. As more and more people fill the Earth, there is less room for wildlife. Humans clear land to put up buildings. They farm land for crops or grazing, or they mine it to produce fuel. Precious wildlife habitats are destroyed.

Here are just some of the animals that are in danger of vanishing forever from the forests and woodlands of this planet.

ENDANGERED ANIMAL	WHERE FOUND
African toad	Tanzania, Africa
Eurasian lynx	Northern Europe and down to eastern Asia
Forest little owl	India
Giant armadillo	South America
Giant panda	China
Leadbeater's possum	Australia
Long-haired spider monkey	Northern South America
Pygmy hog	Southern Asia
Spotted-tailed quoll	Australia
Thin-spined porcupine	Southeast Asia

You can find out more about saving the world's wildlife by visiting the World Wildlife Fund (WWF) at http://www.panda.org.

Glossary

agile lively and active

ambush to attack after waiting in a hiding place

amphibians animals that can live on land and in water

antennae feelers on an animal's head that it uses to smell, touch, or taste

antivenin the medicine given to someone bitten by a venomous animal to stop the venom from hurting them

camouflage something in an animal's appearance that helps it to blend into the background

canine teeth the pointed teeth on each side of the upper and lower jaw

carnivorous meat-eating

colony a group of animals that live close together

deciduous losing leaves every year, usually in fall or winter

dung the droppings of an animal

evergreen having leaves all year round

fangs long, sharp, hollow teeth that are used by snakes to inject venom

food chain the relationship between living things. It shows which animals eat which in order to survive

habitat an animal's natural living place

hibernate to completely rest during winter, often underground

larvae the young of an insect before they start to grow into adults

mammals animals whose young feed on their mother's milk

marsupials mammals that keep and feed their young in a pouch after their birth until they can look after themselves

parasites animals that live and feed on another living animal

predators animals that hunt and kill other animals

prey animals that are caught and eaten by other animals

regurgitate to bring food up from the stomach to the mouth

rodents the group of gnawing or nibbling mammals, such as rats and mice

scats the droppings of an animal

scavengers animals that feed off dead animals

sow a female pig

stalk to follow prey silently until ready to rush out and pounce

suffocation killing by stopping air flow to the lungs, which in turn stops breathing

talons claws, especially for grasping or for attacking

tusks very long teeth that are used in fights and in self defense

venom poison that is injected by some animals to attack their enemies

Index